LET'S RIDE!

MUSCLE CARS

MARIE ROGERS

PowerKids press.

NEW YORK

Published in 2022 by The Rosen Publishing Group, Inc.
29 East 21st Street, New York, NY 10010

First Edition

Portions of this work were originally authored by J. Poolos and published as *Wild About Muscle Cars*. All new material in this edition was authored by Marie Rogers.

Editor: Kate Mikoley
Book Design: Rachel Rising

Photo Credits: Cover Lynch Shannon/Shutterstock.com; Cover, pp. 1, 3, 4, 6, 8, 10, 12, 14, 16, 18, 20, 22, 23, 24 StarLine/Shutterstock.com; Cover. p.1 absemetov/Shutterstock.com; pp. 4, 8,12, 18 schlol/E+/Getty Images; p. 5 peepo/E+/Getty Images; p. 6 YaskoCreative/iStock/Getty Images Plus; p. 7 shaunl/E+/Getty Images; p. 9 sierrarat/E+/Getty Images; p. 10 NosUA/iStock/Getty Images Plus; p. 11 AM-C/E+/Getty Images; p. 13 Tony Savino/Shutterstock.com; p. 14 Heritage Images/Contributor/Hulton Archive/Getty Images; p. 15 Peek Creative Collective/Shutterstock.com; p. 16 Barrett-Jackson/Contributor/Getty Images; p. 17 Barry Blackburn/Shutterstock.com; p. 19 Martyn Goddard/Editorial RF/Getty Images; p. 20 Anadolu Agency/Contributor/Getty Images; p. 21 David McNew/Stringer/Getty Images News/Getty Images.

Some of the images in this book illustrate individuals who are models. The depictions do not imply actual situations or events.

Library of Congress Cataloging-in-Publication Data

Names: Rogers, Marie, 1990- author.
Title: Muscle cars / Marie Rogers.
Description: New York : PowerKids Press, [2022] | Series: Let's ride! |
  Includes index.
Identifiers: LCCN 2020045814 | ISBN 9781725327511 (library binding) | ISBN
  9781725327498 (paperback) | ISBN 9781725327504 (6 pack)
Subjects: LCSH: Muscle cars–Juvenile literature.
Classification: LCC TL147 .R59 2022 | DDC 629.222–dc23
LC record available at https://lccn.loc.gov/2020045814

Manufactured in the United States of America

CPSIA Compliance Information: Batch #CSPK22. For Further Information contact Rosen Publishing, New York, New York at 1-800-237-9932.

Find us on

CONTENTS

BUILT FOR SPEED

The term "muscle car" can be used to talk about many different cars. One thing they all have in common is power. A muscle car is a fast car with a strong engine. Muscle cars were very popular in the United States between the late 1950s and the early 1970s. In recent years, they've made a comeback.

Muscle cars are built for speed. The fastest ones can go from 0 to 60 miles (0 to 97 km) per hour in under 5 seconds!

Muscle cars are often used for drag racing.
This is a race between two cars with special
bodies and engines on a straight track.

Muscle-Car Memories

People have different ideas of what makes a muscle car. Many people say the 1949 Oldsmobile Rocket 88 was the first muscle car. Others say the first true muscle car didn't come along until the American Motors Rambler Rebel came out in 1957.

Muscle cars remained popular through the 1960s. Young drivers liked them because they were powerful, looked cool, and weren't too expensive. However, in the 1970s, gas became much more expensive and muscle cars became much less common.

Muscle cars used a lot of gas, so when gas prices went up, many people stopped wanting to drive them.

SUPERCOOL CARS

Some muscle cars look a bit like regular cars you see on the street. However, some **details** set them apart. Muscle cars have colorful paint, sometimes with a racing stripe on the **hood**. The back wheels have thick, wide tires with little **tread**, called slicks.

When a car goes really fast, air underneath it can weaken the car's **grip** on the road. Some muscle cars have big winglike objects called spoilers to help hold the car to the ground.

As the car moves forward, air moves over the spoiler and presses the car to the road. This gets rid of a lifting force that the air underneath the car causes.

START YOUR ENGINES

Since their beginnings, muscle cars have been known for their big and powerful engines. Over time, these engines have continued to grow even larger and stronger.

Engine power is measured with a unit called horsepower. By the mid-1970s, the engines in muscle cars were commonly making between 350 and 420 horsepower. Today, it's not uncommon for muscle cars to have engines that make around 500 horsepower. Some even make more than 700 horsepower.

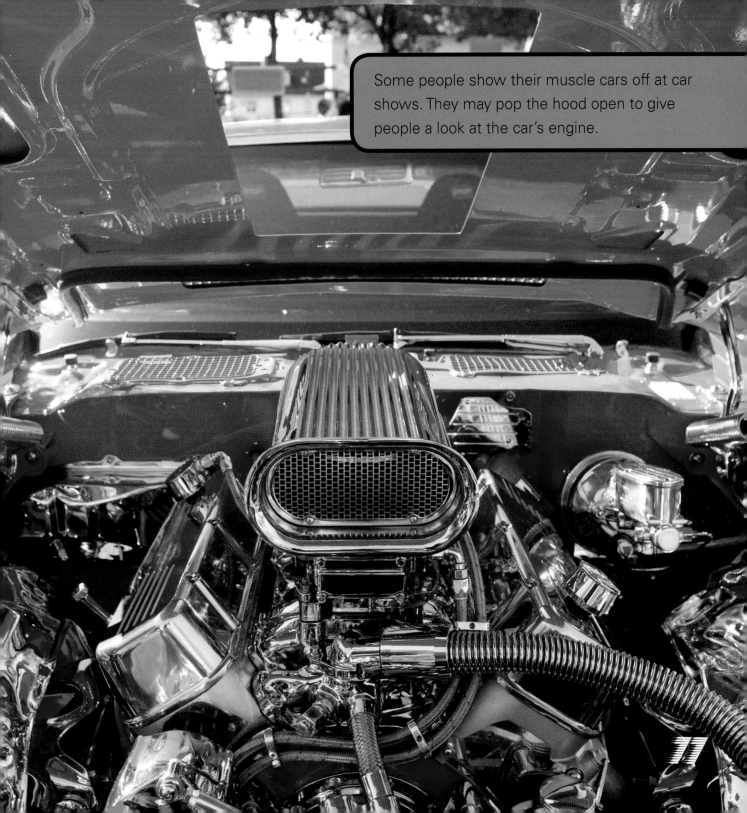

Some people show their muscle cars off at car shows. They may pop the hood open to give people a look at the car's engine.

POPULAR PONTIACS

Most people agree that the cars we now know as muscle cars have existed since at least the late 1950s. However, the term "muscle car" wasn't commonly used until 1964. That year, a magazine writer used the term about a Pontiac GTO.

GTOs quickly became popular. Early models could reach 60 miles (97 km) per hour in about 6 seconds. Later GTOs were even faster. Today, GTOs are still some of the most well-known and well-loved muscle cars.

Old Pontiac GTOs, like this one from 1974, are still popular among muscle-car fans today.

TAKE CHARGE!

After seeing the success of the Pontiac GTO, the carmaker Dodge thought the time was right to make a muscle car of its own. In 1966, it produced the Charger, one of the most famous muscle cars of all time. It was the first American car sold to the public to have a spoiler.

Many muscle-car owners like to soup up their cars, or make changes to make them go even faster. Many early Chargers are still out there today but with new parts!

The Dodge Charger quickly became popular on NASCAR tracks and on the roads. It even appeared in movies and TV shows.

EASY-TO-OPERATE OLDSMOBILES

When it comes to muscle cars, speed is key. But some early muscle cars were so fast they were hard to drive on roads.

The Oldsmobile Cutlass 442 was both fast and easy to drive. Oldsmobile first made the car in 1964. Later, the company improved the cars so they could **compete** with other muscle cars. The 1970 model could go from 0 to 60 miles (0 to 97 km) per hour in 5.7 seconds!

Oldsmobile sometimes called their cars "Youngmobiles" to appeal to young people and get them to buy cars like the 442.

RALLIES AND RACES

By the late 1970s, muscle cars weren't very popular anymore. However, they've made a comeback in recent years! Today, some people buy old muscle cars and **restore** them. They often take them to rallies, or gatherings, for old cars. Some muscle-car fans take part in parades, car shows, and **contests** for the best car.

For some, muscle cars are still all about the speed. They fix their cars so they go really fast and race at drag strips.

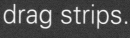

Today, muscle cars are popular in many places around the world. This one is at a show in England.

SRR 117F

19

MUSCLE CARS OF TODAY

When muscle cars became popular again, carmakers started making new ones. Some of today's muscle cars share the same names as old muscle cars, such as the Dodge Charger.

New muscle cars use modern **technology** and are more comfortable than old muscle cars. However, they still have the same cool look as muscle cars of the past. Most importantly, they have powerful engines. Whether buying new or souping up an old model, people sure love their muscle cars!

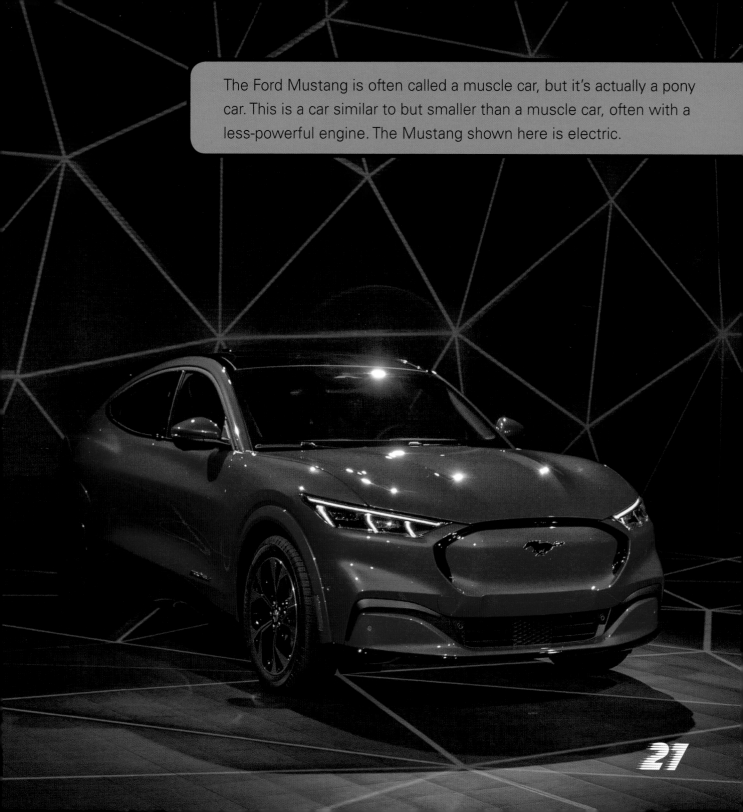

The Ford Mustang is often called a muscle car, but it's actually a pony car. This is a car similar to but smaller than a muscle car, often with a less-powerful engine. The Mustang shown here is electric.

GLOSSARY

compete: To try to win a contest with others.

contest: An event in which people try to win.

detail: A small part of something.

grip: To keep a hold on something.

hood: The cover over a car's engine.

restore: To bring something back to an earlier or better condition.

technology: Using science, engineering, and other industries to invent useful tools or to solve problems. Also a machine, piece of equipment, or method created by technology.

tread: Raised edges on tires that help grip the road.

FOR MORE INFORMATION

BOOKS

Caswell, Deanna. *Muscle Cars*. Mankato, MN: Black Rabbit Books, 2018.

Fishman, Jon M. *Cool Muscle Cars*. Minneapolis, MN: Lerner Publishing Group, 2019.

WEBSITES

History of Cars
www.dkfindout.com/us/transportation/history-cars/
Learn more about different kinds of cars people have driven since the automobile was invented.

What Is a Muscle Car?
wonderopolis.org/wonder/what-is-a-muscle-car
Find more fun facts about muscle cars here.

INDEX